101 CATACLYSMS

FOR THE LOVE OF CATS

EBURY
PRESS

101 CATACLYSMS

FOR THE LOVE OF CATS

RACHAEL HALE

FOR ALL THE CATS
WE LOVE AND CHERISH –

ESPECIALLY EDMUND!

The uninitiated of the human species believe a cat is a cat. Yes, every cat is alike in that they are independent creatures, who come home to eat and sleep before wandering off to do what ever business a cat must do. But it is obvious the unversed have never met a cat like Pat.

Pat is a strapping, black and white domestic short hair – or "moggy" – who lives at my local veterinary clinic. You will find him most days curled up on top of the computer in the clinic, or waiting on the receptionist's swivel chair for someone to give him a whirl. But Pat's real passion is travel, and the sign on the clinic door warns visiting pet owners to thoroughly check their vehicles for the adventurous cat before they drive away.

Soon after I had captured a classic "cool cat" Pat pose for this book, news came of his latest trip – a five-kilometre ride atop a car, the driver oblivious to her passenger, gleefully roof-surfing through busy city streets. I'm certain Pat has been blessed with 18 lives.

Pat is no ordinary feline, but then none of the 101 cats photographed for this book could ever be classed as ordinary.

In my endeavours I have been enlightened, and thoroughly captivated, by clever, nimble, impish, loveable cats – and every one different from the last. While to the untrained eye most cats look alike but for the shape of their eyes or the rich hues of their fur, every cat I have met is a unique individual.

I quickly ascertained there were different ways to work with different breeds. The Persians were funny and floppy, but some of them could also be highly strung.

The Asian cats were often naughty but brimming with character; the Burmese the most mischievous; the Russian Blues shy and unsure of the big outside world; the "moggies" all sweet-natured.

Capturing cats on film was a much more challenging task than photographing dogs. Most of the time, dogs will sit where you ask them to, but you can never pick up a cat, place them on the spot and expect them to stay there. They will always stand up, affronted, and walk straight back to where you fetched them from. I now entice cats with my Hansel and Gretel technique – laying down morsels of food in a trail to where I want them to go. You must possess a vast amount of patience to overcome "feline fickleness". When you finally capture that character and attitude on film, it's worth the hours spent. The trick is to get to know the cat and let them feel they trust you. I would spend hours letting them take their time to approach me, schmooze against my legs and eventually lay claim to my lap. Just one cat put me in my place with a swift swipe of the paw – my only wound after years of photographing animals. After he drew blood, he seemed satisfied that he was in control of the situation, and we got on famously.

Some of the cats displayed incredible tolerance themselves. Nikon, a moggy I have known for many years, was a model of poise and patience. He was chosen to pose with his friend Nigel because of his special gentle nature and even with a mouse on top of his head, he simply stared deep and calmly into the camera lens.

Every photograph was shot in the cat's own environment – in a studio, it would have taken them days to settle. I do my utmost to avoid ever putting animals under stress, or forcing them to do anything against their will, so it was important to choose cats who were comfortable under the spotlight. Some were initially nervous about the big lights and strange camera I would bring along – an imposing 4 x 5 inch large-format camera like an old-fashioned box with the black cape over the back. But, as naturally inquisitive creatures, I would give them time to investigate the equipment.

I have learned so much about my own triumvirate of cats – the roguish Himalayan Persian Edmund, and my designer "moggies" Gianni and Versace – through this mission, and now look at them with a totally new respect.

I definitely believe in the quote "Dogs believe they are human. Cats believe they are God". Cats are so fiercely independent and free spirited, but thank goodness, they still feel the need to humour, protect and make a fuss of us humans every now and again.   RACHAEL HALE

It's one for the money, two for the show,

three to get ready, now go, cat go!

CARL PERKINS, 'BLUE SUEDE SHOES'

1. HOBBIE 2. MINDY 3. TYSON 4. KC DOMESTIC SHORTHAIR AND LONGHAIR

The smallest feline is a masterpiece.

LEONARDO DA VINCI

8. PENELOPE HIGHLAND VARIANT ▶

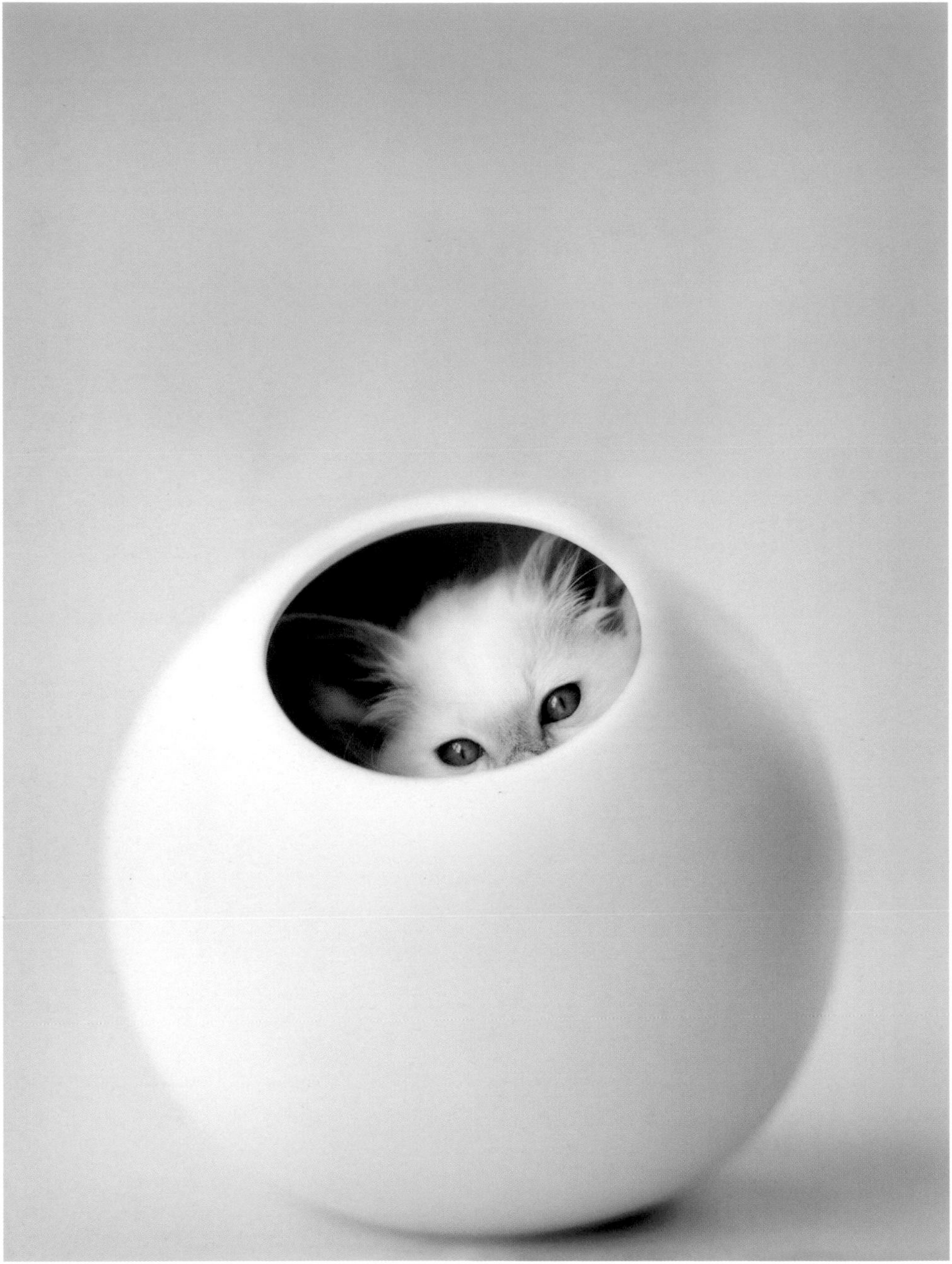

9. ZEN LILAC POINT BALINESE ▼

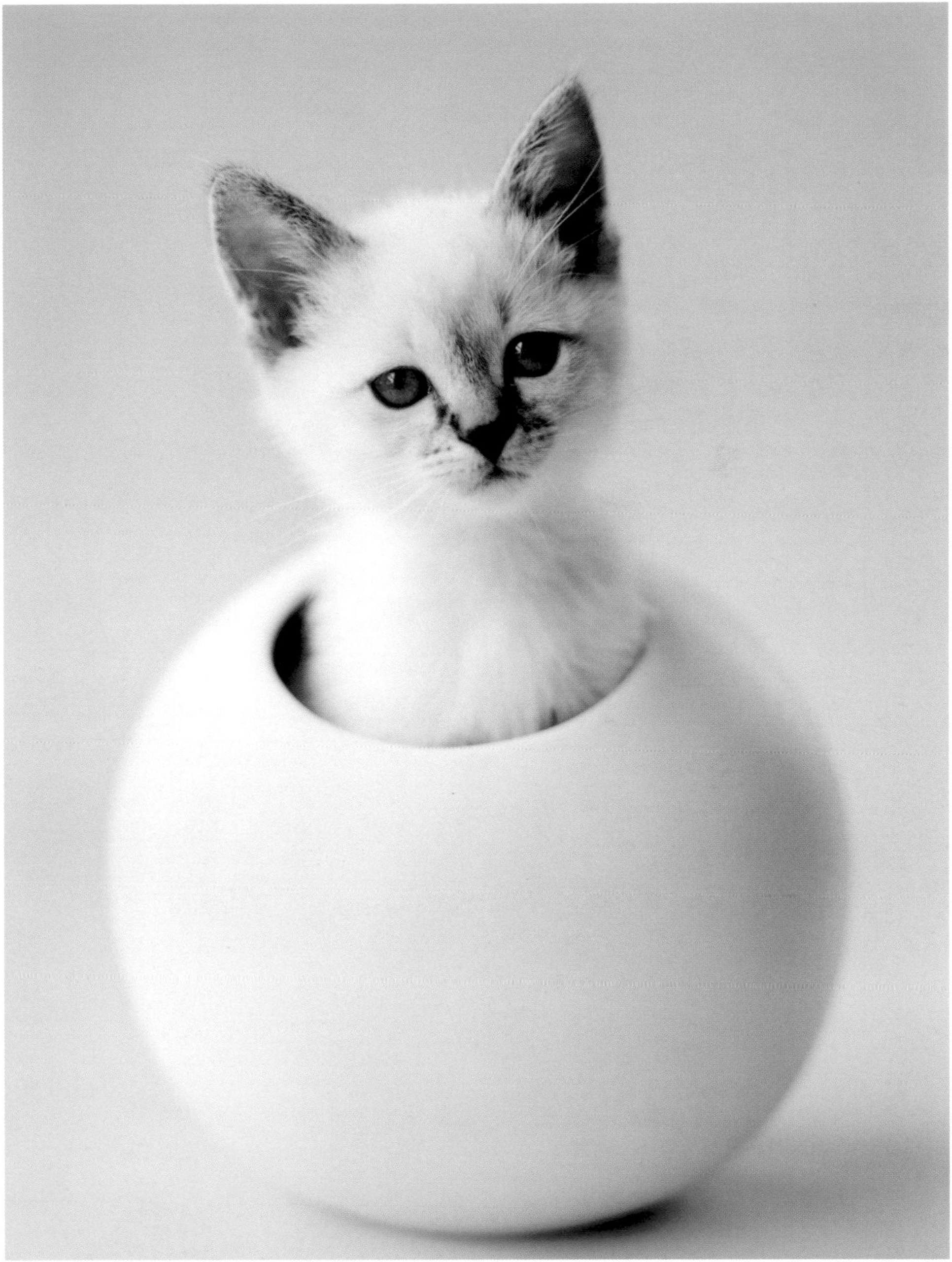

10. WIZARD OF OZ TEMPLE CAT ▼

13 & 14. SUNRISE & DAWN BROWN MARBLED BENGAL ▶

Cats are connoisseurs of comfort.

JAMES HERRIOT

15. YABBA DABBA DOO BLUE POINT BRITISH SHORTHAIR ▶

▲ 17. TOBY LYNX POINT RAGDOLL

Cats are rather delicate creatures

and they are subject to a good many

ailments, but I never heard of one

who suffered from insomnia.

JOSEPH WOOD KRUTCH

BARNABY

21. LILAC BRITISH SHORTHAIR

▲ 23. MARC ANTHONY BIRMAN

24 & 25. GUINESS & FATBOY DOMESTIC SHORTHAIR ▶

No amount of time can erase

the memory of a good cat,

and no amount of masking tape

can ever totally remove his

fur from your couch.

LEO DWORKEN

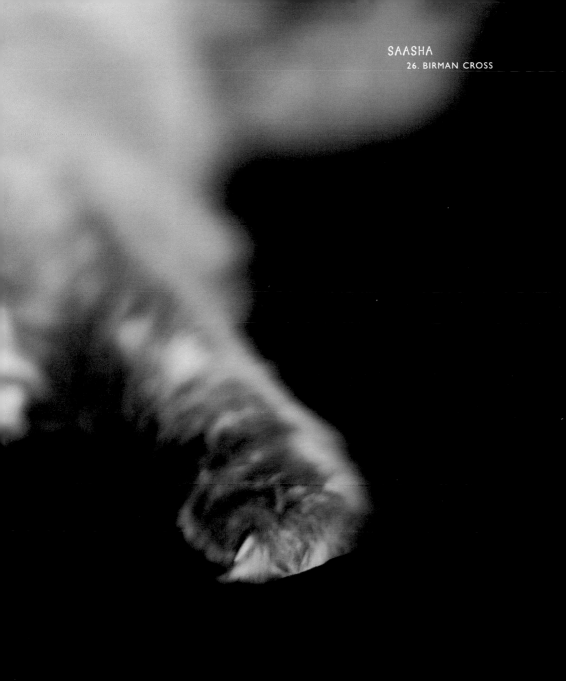

RAMSEY

29. TRINITY RUSSIAN BLUE CROSS ▶

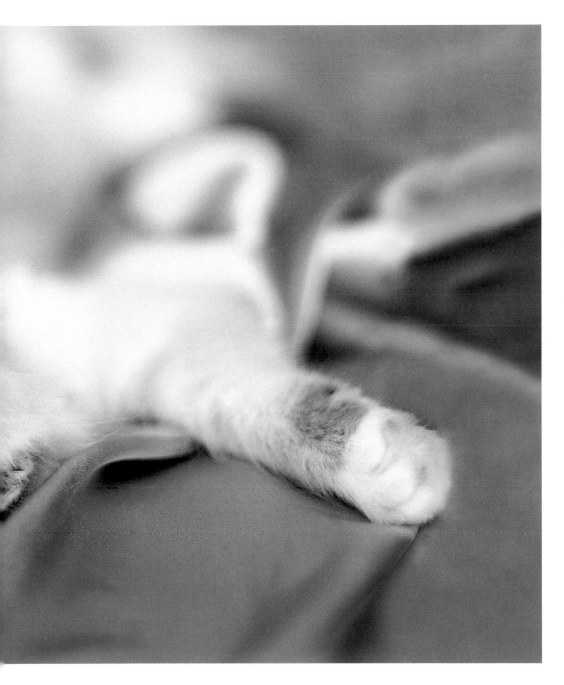

To bathe a cat takes

brute force, perseverance,

courage of conviction — and a cat.

The last ingredient is usually

hardest to come by.

STEPHEN BAKER

EDMUND

32. HIMALAYAN PERSIAN ▶

◄ 33. RASCAL CHOCOLATE PERSIAN

We looked!

Then we saw him step on the mat!

We looked!

And we saw him!

The Cat in the Hat!

DR SEUSS

36. GUINESS DOMESTIC SHORTHAIR ▶

MERLIN

40. SCOTTISH FOLD

Cat people are different,

to the extent that they

generally are not conformists.

How could they be,

with a cat running their lives?

LOUIS J CAMUTI

VENEZIA
◄ 41. BROWN TABBY TIFFANIE

CHLOE

◀ 43. DOMESTIC LONGHAIR

TEDDY

44. RED TABBY EXOTIC ▶

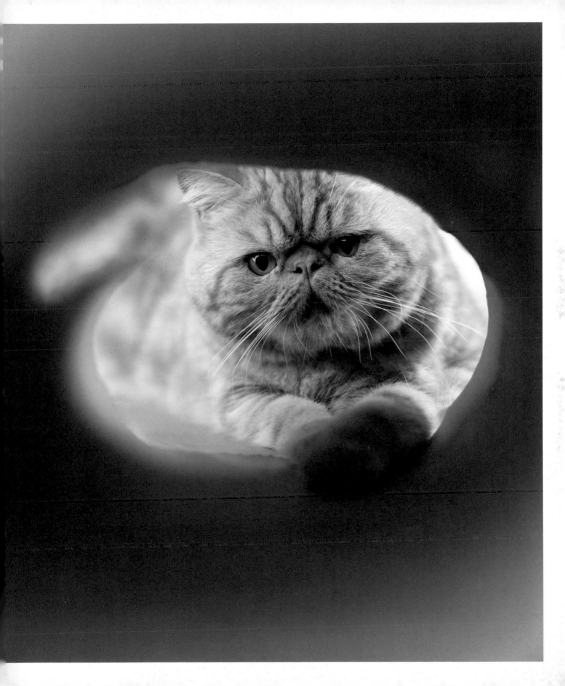

TOSCANO

◀ 45. ASIAN SHORTHAIR

Cat: A pygmy lion

who loves mice, hates dogs,

and patronizes human beings.

OLIVER HERFORD

▲ 47. GOKU DOMESTIC SHORTHAIR

WINNIE

48. DOMESTIC TABBY ▶

▲ 50. LU-LU BROWN SPOTTED BENGAL

BIG BOY PUSS

◀ 51. ISLE OF MAN

When she walked… she

stretched out long and thin like

a little tiger, and held her head

high to look over the grass as if

she were treading the jungle.

SARAH ORNE JEWETT

▲ 54. BLACK ELLE EBONY ORIENTAL

CROSBY

◀ 55. CYMRIC

Prowling his own quiet backyard or

asleep by the fire, he is still only a

whisker away from the wilds.

JEAN BURDEN

TIN TIN

◀ 59. RUDDY ABYSSINIAN

If man could be crossed with a

cat it would improve man, but

it would deteriorate the cat.

MARK TWAIN

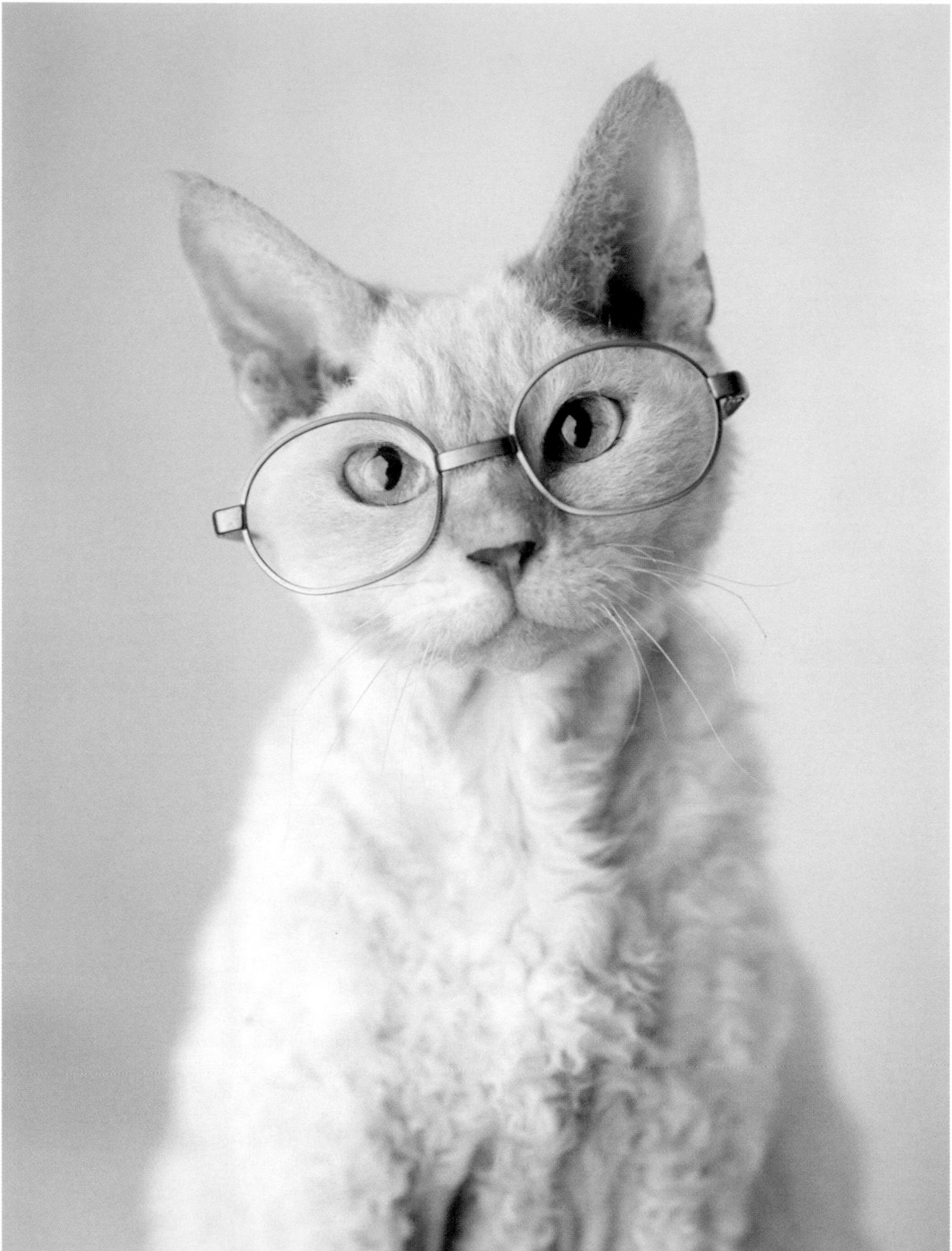

61. KANGO DEVON REX ◀

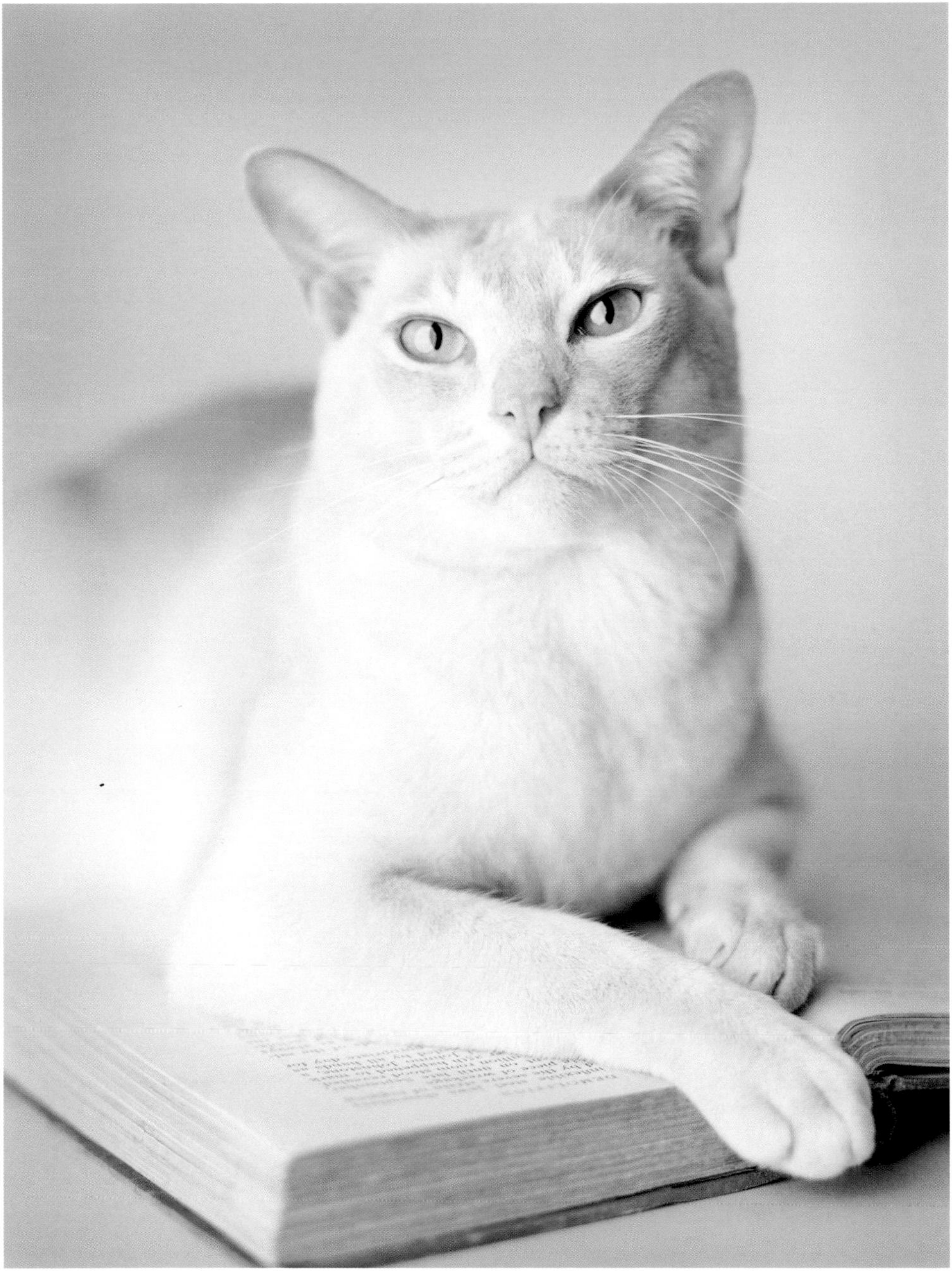

62. CIAREN CREAM BURMESE ▼

A kitten is chiefly remarkable

for rushing about like mad

at nothing whatsoever, and

generally stopping before it gets there.

AGNES REPPLIER

◄ 63. SCRUFFY DOMESTIC SHORTHAIR

◄ 64. BLACK KNIGHT BRITISH SHORTHAIR

65. JEZITA BURMILLA ▶

Pussycat, pussycat, you're so thrilling

and I'm so willing, to care for you. . .

Pussycat, Pussycat, I love you!

TOM JONES, 'WHAT'S NEW PUSSYCAT'

▲ 69. WILLOW COLOUR POINT TABBY RAGDOLL

▲ 70. MISTY MITTED TABBY RAGDOLL

▲ 72. CASPER BLUE POINT BRITISH SHORTHAIR

It is with the approach

of winter that cats…

wear their richest fur and

assume an air of sumptuous

and delightful opulence.

PIERRE LOTI

73. NEVADA SILVER SHADED PERSIAN ▶

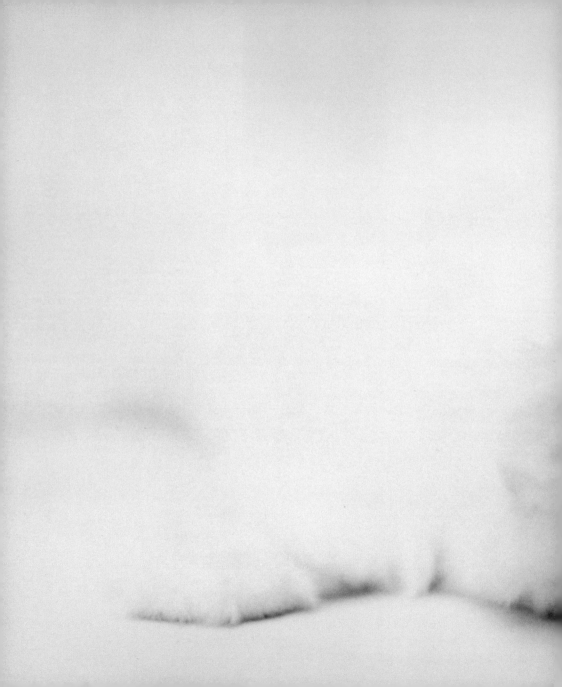

74. KASPAR SILVER SHADED PERSIAN

76. SARA TONKINESE ▶

Dogs believe they are human.

Cats believe they are God.

ANON

◀ 78. PAT THE CAT DOMESTIC SHORTHAIR

HILANDER

◀ 79. SPHYNX

▲ 81. MR SMEEGALL SEAL BURMESE

TAHLULLAH

82. BOMBAY

NIKON & NIGEL

◀ 83. ABYSSINIAN CROSS

The owl and the pussy-cat went to sea,

In a beautiful pea-green boat;

They took some honey, and plenty of money,

Wrapped up in a five-pound note.

EDWARD LEAR

HONEY

85. RAGDOLL CROSS ▶

DIESEL

◄ 86. LYNX POINT SIAMESE

▲ 88. BAD BOY BOB CORNISH REX

REX

Even a cat is a lion in her own lair.

INDIAN PROVERB

90. CAIRO EGYPTIAN MAU ▶

▲ 92. KIRBY DOMESTIC MEDIUM HAIR

MCGUIVER
◄ 93. DOMESTIC SHORTHAIR

94. VADAR CHOCOLATE SHADED BURMILLA ▼

▲ 95. JESSIE JAVANESE

REUBEN JAMES

96. FAWN POINT BALINESE ▶

Thou art the Great Cat,

the avenger of the Gods

and the judge of words,

and the president of the sovereign chiefs

and the governor of the holy Circle;

thou art indeed... the Great Cat.

INSCRIPTION ON THE ROYAL TOMBS AT THEBES

99. STAR SILVER CLASSIC TABBY MAINE COON ▶

100 + 1

100/101. BASBOUSCHKA & CHARISMA BROWN SPOTTED TABBY BENGAL ▶

INDEX

It was a challenge to grab the attention of a gang of kittens intent on sliding down the smooth fabric. But perseverance and patience with animals always pays off – even if Tyson was caught off guard!

He may have played along, but Sapphire made it obvious he was not impressed at hanging in a sling. He would not offer a smile – just a catty smirk.

Zoe was a cat acrobat, leaping through the air, scaling walls, trying to master the tightrope and snatch the feather toy as quick as a wink, so I had to be swift with the shutter to catch her the right way up.

He may have been barely four weeks old, but this little guy was born with a strong will – he was determined not to sit still on a human hand. After much wriggling, Maximus exhausted himself, and had no choice but to snuggle down and take a nap.

Like a graceful ballerina, Penelope turned pirouette after pirouette trying to catch a clutch of feathers, and paused for but a brief moment, mesmerised by her prey.

Little Zen, shy and coy, was encouraged to take a peek from his hiding place with a little sweet talking.

Unlike Zen, Wizard of Oz was a jack in the box, so we had to work fast! My assistant had to keep her hand over the hole to stop him from immediately leaping out.

This pair enjoyed hanging around in matching stockings, being entertained by flying feathers. But it wasn't long before they figured out how to wriggle out and capture them.

Bengal kittens are full of mischief and boundless energy, so the best way to keep this bouncy pair in hand was to swathe them together in soft fabric and suspend them gently off the ground.

Yabba Dabba Doo was happy to be put in a pocket to be photographed – it turned out to be the perfect way to keep a rascally kitten still.

It's not often you get to work with a tiny, fragile three-week-old kitten, and credit must be given to Vivaldi's breeder, who gently stroked him to sleep in the little box so we could capture this magical image of a sleeping beauty.

Ragdolls – so floppy and flexible – were perfect cats for this image, and I had five of them taking turns dozing in the little hammock. It was Toby who stole the show with his classic Ragdoll flop.

My own "designer moggies" – brothers and bundles of trouble. Just because their mum is the photographer doesn't mean they are born models. I captured just two images of the terrors before they dashed back into the garden.

20.
FOREIGN WHITE ORIENTAL
Cupcake – 10 weeks old

Despite an exhausting game of chase, Cupcake was determined not to fall asleep amongst the dessert. We had to fool her with a box placed over the dish before she fell into a deep slumber, unmoved by the aroma of fresh cupcakes.

21.
LILAC BRITISH SHORTHAIR
Barnaby – nine weeks old

After a morning frolicking with his kitten friends, Barnaby curled up to sleep in his soft fleecy blanket. A little tickle under his chin in his catnap, and he fashioned a lazy smile.

22.
PERSIAN
Dreamy Lace – 10 years old

This cat and I have a long and successful working relationship. Every time I photograph her, she closes her eyes It isn't hard to capture an image of her sleeping – even though I know she is wide awake under those heavy lids!

23.
BIRMAN
Marc Anthony – eight weeks old

Who wouldn't fall asleep with a smile on their face, after being gently patted and placed on a soft bed of silk?

24 & 25.
DOMESTIC SHORTHAIR
Guiness and Fatboy – eight weeks old

It took a few hours of patient waiting while these cat brothers raced around. Finally there was no energy left and they collapsed in a contented sleep, curled together inside a bowl.

26.
BIRMAN CROSS
Saasha – 11 years old

This cat has style and a penchant for classy accessories – she puts up a mean fight to keep visitors' handbags and shoes. Saasha is also a real smoocher and loved basking in the sun on black velvet.

27.
CYMRIC
Ramsey – eight years old

Ramsey was not the least bit interested in me when we first met – she was far too busy stalking prey out in the bushes. But on her day before the camera, she was the model of tolerance and good manners.

28.
TIFFANIE
Danielle – three and a half years old

When I first met the magisterial Danielle, she was serving "time out" – sent to her room for bossing around the other cats in the household. When we met again, she was on her best behaviour for the lens.

29.
RUSSIAN BLUE CROSS
Trinity – four years old

Mixed with the affection and intelligence of this cat is a hint of attitude. As I was leaning in to take this shot, Trinity reached out a paw as if we were communicating in our own special language.

30.
RAGDOLL
Angel – three months old

Angel was a perfect example of a Ragdoll – totally relaxed and floppy. But little did her owners know she would grow up to be an explorer, roaming the neighbourhood on her next adventure.

31.
DOMESTIC TABBY
Cougar – two years old

Swimming may be rare behaviour for a cat, but Cougar eagerly dived into a tub of warm suds. His keenness was heightened by the promise of a treat, so he was oblivious to the bubbles bobbing around him.

32.
HIMALAYAN PERSIAN
Edmund – four and a half months old

Ed, my beloved crazy cat, is a gutter snipe – happy to nap in the drains along our street. Understandably, he needs bathing often – this was his first plunge at four months old.

33.
CHOCOLATE PERSIAN
Rascal – nine weeks old

This is one of my favourite photos. Knowing Rascal is always a rascal, it was no surprise he spent most of the time spinning around in the vase chasing his tail.

34.
PERSIAN
Baronosski – 10 years old

Baronosski is a champion show cat, so taking a bath before showing his best side to the camera was second nature for him.

35.
CHOCOLATE BURMESE
Chino – 18 months old

Unlike most cats – especially the spirited Burmese – Chino was a little unsure of the drift of feathers circling his head, but his innate curiosity eventually got the better of him.

36.
DOMESTIC SHORTHAIR
Guiness – two years old

Never let anyone say you can't pull the wool over a cat's eyes! Guiness is an incredibly tolerant cat who will wear his beanie at a jaunty angle – even if it means he cannot see a thing!

37 & 38.
RUSSIAN BLUE
Alexei and Cossak – eight weeks old

Russian Blues are shy, quiet cats, and when Alexei and Cossak had their first experience out in the big, wide world, they became cat contortionists, timidly backing into the far reaches of the box.

39.
DOMESTIC LONGHAIR
Vincent – four years old

Vincent wore an air of sophistication, complemented by his blue fur cap and stole. It was not difficult to persuade this gentleman to pose for the camera.

40.
SCOTTISH FOLD
Merlin – eight weeks old

This busy little magician ran around the house for hours with his wizard cap on, refusing to come to a halt until sleep descended on him – fortunately with the hat still balanced on his head.

41.
BROWN TABBY TIFFANIE
Venezia – 10 weeks old

It was a difficult lesson learned when five kittens were introduced to the intoxication of crumpled newspaper. Venezia was the only one among them who sat still for the single minute needed to capture her portrait.

42.
DOMESTIC SHORTHAIR
Clayton – six months old

It was a case of the country cat comes to the city, and Clayton, who lives in a farmyard barn, brought his best manners with him. The cat with the incredible eyes placed his paws exactly where asked – even inside the foreign territory of a city shopping bag.

43.
DOMESTIC LONGHAIR
Chloe – 10 years old

The Hansel and Gretel technique – food laid out in a strategic trail – was invented for Chloe, who performed perfectly once she realised there was a reward at the end of the box.

44.
RED TABBY EXOTIC
Teddy – two years old

Teddy could have been straight out of the cartoon strip Garfield – what a character! Although we wanted him inside the roll of paper, he decided he wanted a reversal of roles, and got the camera in there instead.

45.
ASIAN SHORTHAIR
Toscano – six months old

This is one hilarious, curious cat. If there was no sign of Toscano, you only had to look in the film bag, or the light case… or in, under and over anything. It seemed perfectly natural to capture him discovering somewhere new.

46.
SILVER TABBY EXOTIC
Buster – three years old

Buster, a cat infamous for stealing his neighbours' hairbrushes, wins the award for the longest shoot. He was happy to play with us all day, but it took him seven hours to get the gist of staring down the lens.

47.
DOMESTIC SHORTHAIR
Goku – six months old

The sweetest-natured cat I have ever caught on film, Goku spent as much time cuddling and cavorting as he did getting down to business. He would cock his head like a dog when listening to directions.

48.
DOMESTIC TABBY
Winnie – three and a half years old

Intrigued as I photographed his housemate Goku, Winnie demanded a taste of the limelight. This shot was captured between his attempts to whip off with the cream on freshly-baked scones in the kitchen.

49.
SEAL LYNX ORIENTAL
Jenny Any Dots – four months old

This tiny little kitten – so fragile, yet so robust and full of energy – revelled in the chance to tangle with the usually forbidden basket of wool.

50.
BROWN SPOTTED BENGAL
Lu-lu – nine weeks old

Lu-lu is a sweet wee girl, but full of kittenish antics. She sat still just long enough for her bold Bengal spots not to become a blur.

51.
ISLE OF MAN
Big Boy Puss – three years old

The cat otherwise known as B.B. Puss was a border at a cattery I was visiting, and no one could ignore a face that exuded such charm and character.

52.
ASIAN LEOPARD
Naomi – 11 years old

Looks can deceive – Naomi has the face of a wildcat, but she is gentle and loving. She would stalk through the long grass towards the chicken coop, from where we would retrieve her so she could do it all over again.

53.
LAVENDER MANDALAY
Jenny Lavender – three years old

It required much persuasion to get Jenny Lavender to sit amongst her fragrant namesake flowers – the strong scent simply did not appeal to her. She even refused her favourite meal of liver, but was lured to the spot with tiny titbits of cheese.

54.
EBONY ORIENTAL
Black Elle – two years old

Strange as it may sound, Black Elle loves to pick a bouquet of flowers from the garden and carry them around in her mouth. Of course, she would not do this for the camera, but she was happy to pose surrounded by her treasured blooms.

55.
CYMRIC
Crosby – 12 years old

Crosby can proudly claim to be the only cat who gave me a war wound. With a swift swipe of claws across my wrist, establishing who was boss, he had no problem lying on the warm pebbles – like his favourite spot atop the concrete water tank at home.

56.
SEAL BURMESE
Errol – six years old

It's no wonder this cat goes by the name Feral Errol, drawing blood from his owner's cheek and leg during the shoot. But to show there was no hard feelings, the following morning Errol delivered a gift of wild rabbit to the foot of the bed.

57.
MAINE COON
Romeo – one year old

If I was cat, I would have found my Romeo. Handsome, gentle and with a heart of gold, this Romeo was happy to do whatever was asked of him.

58.
NORWEGIAN FOREST CAT
Carl – two and a half years old

Thrilled by a new twig to tease, it took this forest cat some time before he stopped cavorting and posed in his own majestic style.

59.

RUDDY ABYSSINIAN

Tin Tin – six months old

Even though Abyssinians are celebrated hunters, Tin Tin was enthralled at being "captured" in a net, entertained by cat toys.

60.

SNOW MARBLED BENGAL

Castello – 10 weeks old

This little guy would do anything for a tummy rub, and was happy to lie back on my assistant's lap and purr for the camera.

61.

DEVON REX

Kango – six years old

Kango is one cool cat who did not mind donning glasses – perhaps it even helped him focus on the morsels of meat dangled above the lens.

62.

CREAM BURMESE

Ciaren – six years old

My "Mr Cruise" lay anywhere but where I wanted him – on the book. He was eventually persuaded with the tactical placing of treats on the fold and a much appreciated rub under the chin.

63.

DOMESTIC SHORTHAIR

Scruffy – eight and a half weeks old

Scruffy is a tiny guy with an enormous personality. He was adopted from an animal welfare centre and taken to a loving new home, where he caused chaos and destruction. I guess being so little, means you can get away with a lot.

64.

BRITISH SHORTHAIR

Black Knight – 11 weeks old

Amongst a cute kindle of kittens, it was only Black Knight who boldly stepped forward to the lens. He was so laid back and co-operative, the perfect image was captured in a matter of minutes.

65.

BURMILLA

Jezita – three months old

Kittens can squeeze into the most remarkable spaces, like between the bars of a birdcage. Jezita was fooled by our feather teaser into thinking she had snared the prize.

66.

LYNX BI-COLOUR RAGDOLL

Dexter – seven weeks old

From the word go, Dexter was the little troublemaker in his tribe – the youngest, smallest and naughtiest of five Ragdoll kittens. The moment his siblings snuggled down to sleep, Dexter would pounce.

67 & 68.

DOMESTIC SHORTHAIR

Samuel and Suzy – eight weeks old

These two mischievous cats were mesmerised by a feather on the end of a stick – before they discovered how to scramble out of the vase.

69.

COLOUR POINT TABBY RAGDOLL

Willow – nine weeks old

Willow was content to lie totally relaxed on her pedestal bed, while we wrestled with the other kittens who were trying to snatch the cat toys we waved about to keep the subject awake.

70.

MITTED TABBY RAGDOLL

Misty – nine weeks old

It was a tight squeeze to get this little tabby Ragdoll inside the vase – she had grown so much in the two weeks since I first met her! It became all too obvious that my plan to get two kittens in there would never see the light of day.

71.

CREAM POINT PERSIAN

Puffy – six months old

It was love at first sight when I met Puffy, a debonair fellow with cheeks of blushed apricot. The challenge was to stop him hiding his natural good looks as he burrowed under the cosy blanket.

72.

BLUE POINT BRITISH SHORTHAIR

Casper – five weeks old

Three little bundles of fluff tried out for this image, but it was Casper who artfully draped a limb over the lip of the jug, while the others got lost inside.

73.
SILVER SHADED PERSIAN
Nevada – five years old

Nevada hails from the chilly climes of 46 degrees south and is used to the cold, but still loved snuggling into the warm fur tube.

74.
SILVER SHADED PERSIAN
Kaspar – six years old

Kaspar has the largest eyes I have ever seen on a cat, and he has huge paws, a big gentle nature and a mighty laid-back attitude to match. He lolled about, happy to be entertained.

75.
DOMESTIC MEDIUM HAIR
Charlie – two years old

The last cat to be photographed for the book, Charlie was adopted by my friends to soften the recent loss of their beloved Newfoundland dog, George. Charlie immediately took charge of his new home, bossing everyone around, including my 80kg Newfoundland, Henry.

76.
TONKINESE
Sara – four years old

Sara took a break from napping, nuzzled into the side of her closest buddy, a Rhodesian Ridgeback named Azizi, to pose nonchalantly for the camera.

77.
KORAT
Oscar – three years old

This was a one-shot wonder. Oscar, the stud cat, spent most of the time rubbing against everything in the room. Fortunately, in his quest for another new surface, he ventured under the mesh and peered out for just a split-second.

78.
DOMESTIC SHORTHAIR
Pat the Cat – six years old

Cool cat Pat is often found taking a ride in (or on top of) stranger's cars. But he's just as happy on stable ground as long as there's plenty of human attention – hence this shot with a pat on the head.

79.
SPHYNX
Hilander – nine months old

There is something fantastical about a hairless cat, but Hilander instantly won my heart. He may have felt a little strange to pat but like a genuine Sphynx, he was playful and fun.

80.
RED SELF PERSIAN
Charlotte – eight years old

A fluffy bundle of cuddles and cat kisses, Charlotte is the most affectionate feline I've ever met, with the cutest squeak of a meow that melts your heart.

81.
SEAL BURMESE
Mr Smeegall – seven months old

Burmese are the most adventurous and gregarious cats and a great challenge to capture on film. To contain Mr Smeegall's zeal, he was lured inside a cardboard box by a feather toy waggled in front of his nose.

82.
BOMBAY
Tahlullah – seven and a half years old

The slinky Tahlullah may be stone deaf, but she is not dumb. She could never be shut out while other cats were being photographed – with an uncanny ability to open doors then muscle her feline rivals out of the way.

83.
ABYSSINIAN CROSS
Nikon (and Nigel) – 12 years old

Nikon is a gentle giant of a cat who did not flicker a whisker with brave Nigel perched on his head (and the mouse even left his "calling card" there).

84.
DOMESTIC TABBY
Cougar – two years old

Cougar, the famous water-loving cat, was content to sit in a light shower, as long as he was protected by a doll's raincoat and hat.

85.
RAGDOLL CROSS
Honey – two years old

So as not to risk Honey being stung, we collected bees that had died naturally in their hive, and attached them to her coat using double-sided tape.

86.
LYNX POINT SIAMESE
Diesel – 10 months old

One of the most striking cats I have had the pleasure to photograph, Diesel was also a breeze to work with. He would pose, jump off his old tin drum, let out a classic Siamese yowl, then leap back up again for more.

87.
CORNISH REX
Yoda – four months old

Apparently, Yoda's daily "crazy time" ends at 11am, but in front of the camera it took him a little longer to slow down to anything less than a blur. His spirit made me fall in love with the Cornish Rex breed.

88.
CORNISH REX
Bad Boy Bob – two years old

The name suggests a wayward cat, yet Bad Boy Bob was long, lean, fast, cheeky and adorable – but never bad. All the same, he wasn't keen to hang around for long.

89.
DEVON REX
Rex – 10 weeks old

Cradling Rex in tender hands was the perfect way to show off his remarkable soft and almost furless coat. He reminds me of ET, my favourite movie character as a child.

90.
EGYPTIAN MAU
Cairo – two and a half years old

After lugging 30 concrete blocks up to a third floor apartment to create our set, we sat back and watched Cairo and her pal Rameses investigate their new playground. Before the lens, Cairo showed all the elegance and beauty of an Egyptian queen.

91.
SOMALI
Monty – three years old

Abyssinians are a real handful and the Somali (the long haired version), is just as active and demanding, but a little more laidback…. or maybe that's just Monty, a perfect gentleman.

92.
DOMESTIC MEDIUM HAIR
Kirby – eight years old

Kirby quivered by the cat door, then hid behind the couch, before being cajoled by two cat-mates – and a few little treats and comforting caresses – to join in the fun.

93.
DOMESTIC SHORTHAIR
McGuiver – 15 years old

The oldest cat to grace this book, McGuiver felt his dignity was dented by having to pose for the camera. But the veteran could not hide a frivolous past – as a youth he thought he could fly by leaping out a second storey window.

94.
CHOCOLATE SHADED BURMILLA
Vadar – one year old

The first session of this shoot had to be postponed when Vadar unexpectedly went out for a walk along one of the city's busiest streets. This urban feline takes everything in his stride, and when he was ready he was happy to pose in his owner's apartment.

95.
JAVANESE
Jessie – one year old

Javanese cats are fearless with an insatiable curiosity and Jessie was in her element hanging off the curtains. She would have played for hours entangled in the mesh, had we not convinced her we had homes of our own to go to.

96.
FAWN POINT BALINESE
Reuben James – 10 months old

Reuben James simply claimed the box we had made for him. Although he barely moved a muscle, his soft coat was so thick and luxuriant there was fawn hair flying everywhere around the set!

97 & 98.
OCICAT
Charlie and Josie – one year old

These intelligent but mischievous siblings had been taught to sit on command, but they were yet to learn to stay. It became a mission to stop Charlie bringing his favourite toy, a large wooden spoon, into the frame.

99.
SILVER CLASSIC TABBY MAINE COON
Star – five months old

Star is a strong, serene and magnificent specimen who deserved her place on the pedestal. Maine Coons are large cats (myth has it they were bred from raccoons!), and our tiny Bengal kitten, Lu-lu, was just a quarter of Star's size, although not far apart in age.

100 & 101.
BROWN SPOTTED TABBY BENGAL
Basbouschka and Charisma – 5 weeks old

I love the way cats curl up together in sleep. As if by instinct, Basbouschka and Charisma coiled themselves into the yin and yang position, and fell into a deep, blissful slumber.

It has taken a team effort to produce *101 Cataclysms*, and unfortunately it is impossible to mention and thank every individual. But I am extremely grateful to everyone who helped me turn this project into such an achievement.

Firstly, I would like to thank the two assistants I had while making this book; Nathalie Giacomelli and Charlotte Anderson. You both gave me endless patience and enthusiasm, two attributes that are absolute necessities when working with cats.

My business partners, David and Tanya Todd, also deserve special thanks for their invaluable support and encouragement over the years – allowing me to be as creative as I can be.

Thank you to the other members of our team in New Zealand, especially Robine Harris (design and retouching) and Sandra Seton, along with Richard Horton (UK and Europe) and Eric Kuskey (USA). You have all contributed so much – not only to our last two books, but with many other projects to date, and no doubt, in the future.

Once again, Geoff Blackwell and Ruth-Anna Hobday of PQ Publishers, have given me the freedom that all artists dream of – to be able to create images so close to my heart. Your dedication and support is invaluable and it is thanks to you that these images are shared with people around the world. To Jenny and Kylie, your effort with the production and design of *101 Cataclysms* is greatly appreciated. Thank you to the rest of the team at PQ for being so wonderful to work with. Thanks also to Suzanne McFadden for helping me put into words my descriptions of the images.

This book would not have been possible without my good friends, Rae and John Field. Not only were they always there with a hot cup of tea after a long day's shoot, but they looked after my beloved Newfoundland, Henry, while I was out "capturing" cats. Sadly, Henry's best pal George, the Fields' Newfoundland, passed away near the completion of *101 Cataclysms*. The hole in their lives was soon filled by the adoption of a cat called Charlie, who would become a star of this book. Unfortunately, the arrival of Charlie did not impress Henry, who simply wanted his old buddy back.

Thanks also to the team at Onewa Road Veterinary Clinic in Auckland, especially Richard Lucy who introduced me to so many wonderful cats.

I am also grateful to Image Centre (scanning), PCL (colour print processing), Labtec (black and white print processing) and Apix for their fast, efficient service in delivering my film, especially on the days I had left it to the last minute.

And of course an ENORMOUS thanks to all the cats and their owners for allowing me to capture the essence of these fabulous felines on film.

My final thanks goes to all my friends and family, who constantly support and encourage me, especially my parents, Bob and Barbara, and my twin sister, Rebecca, who are always thrilled to see new images and to offer an opinion. I love you all heaps, and again hope I have made you proud.

Rachael.

The publisher is grateful for literary permissions to reproduce those items below subject to copyright. Every effort has been made to trace the copyright holders and the publisher apologises for any unintentional omission. We would be pleased to hear from any not acknowledged here and undertake to make all reasonable efforts to include the appropriate acknowledgement in any subsequent editions. Extract from How to Live with a Neurotic Cat by Stephen Baker, Copyright © 1985 by Stephen Baker and Jackie Geyer, reproduced with permission from Warner Books, Inc. Extract from The Cat in the Hat TM & Copyright © 1957 Dr. Seuss Enterprises, L.P. All Rights Reserved. (UK and British Commonwealth). Extract from The Cat in the Hat by Dr. Seuss, TM and Copyright © by Dr. Seuss Enterprises, L.P. 1957, renewed 1985. Used by permission of Random House Children's Books, a division of Random House, Inc. (USA and world excluding UK).

First published under licence from Rachael Hale Photography Limited in 2004 by PQ Publishers Limited. This edition published in 2006 by Ebury Publishing, a division of The Random House Group.

1 3 5 7 9 10 8 6 4 2

Ebury Publishing, Random House UK Limited,
20 Vauxhall Bridge Road, London SW1V 2SA

The Random House Group Limited Reg. No. 954009
www.randomhouse.co.uk

A CIP catalogue record for this book is available from the British Library.

Designed by Kylie Nicholls
Text by Suzanne McFadden

Printed by Everbest Printing International Ltd, China

ISBN 0091913659

ISBN-13 (from January 2007) 9780091913656